HEADLINES

HEADLINES

Bilingual poems inspired by fragments of headlines featured in The New York Times

Gabriel Rosenstock

REVIVAL PRESS

LIMERICK - IRELAND

Copyright © Gabriel Rosenstock 2024
First published in Ireland by
Revival Press
Limerick, Ireland

Revival Press is the poetry imprint of
The Limerick Writers' Centre
c/o The Umbrella Project,
78 O'Connell Street, Limerick, Ireland

www.limerickwriterscentre.com
www.facebook.com/limerickwriterscentre

All rights reserved
No part of this publication may be reproduced or transmitted in any form or by any means, electronic or mechanical without permission in writing from the publisher, except by a reviewer who may quote brief passages in a review.

Book Design: Lotte Bender
Cover Image: *Stone figure of a monkey | Limestone | Ancient Egypt, Late New Kingdom, 2nd millennium BC | The Hunt Collection | PD*

Poetry Editor Revival Press: Tommy Collins
Managing Editor LWC: Dominic Taylor

ISBN 978-1-7395610-7-9

Available as an e-book at www.smashwords.com/limerickwriterscentre
Print copy: www.limerickwriterscentre.com

The fragments of headlines from The New York Times used here are considered *fair use* under the copyright act as it is for the purposes of commentary and criticism.

ACIP catalogue number for this publication is available from The British Library

Viva Infrarrealismo!

A homage to *Infrarrealismo*, founded in the mid-1970s by a group of 20 poets in Mexico City: **'to blow the brains out of the cultural establishment.'**

Headlines from the *New York Times* act as a springboard for bilingual poems in this book inspired by the Infras. Period covered: 11th August - 31st August 2023

11th August 2023 also marks the birth of Infrearéalachas, the Irish-language version of Infrarealism.

Contents

Miami and the Rising Seas   10
*Deir Miami go mBeidh sé in ann Déileáil
le hArdú na bhFarraigí*   11

Legal Bills and Trump Cash Crunch   12
*Billí dlíodóirí ag ardú agus Trump i sáinn ó
thaobh airgead reatha de*   13

Fund to Vacuum Greenhouse Gases   14
*Caithfidh SAM $1.2 billiún chun gás ceaptha teasa a
fholúsghlanadh den spéir*   15

Wagner Group, Ready for Coup   16
An Grupa Wagner reidh i gcónaí le haghaidh coup   17

First Russian Spacecraft for Fifty Years Headed to the Moon   18
*Den chéad uair le leathchéad bliain anuas nach mór, tá spásárthach
lainseáilte ag an Rúis agus í ag triall ar an nGealach*   19

Hawaii to Reinvent Itself after 2023 Wildfires   20
Tar éis an uafáis is an dobróin, athróidh Hávái í féin ó bhonn   21

A New Era of Inexpensive Add-On Assault Weapons Spawned   22
Breiseán neamhchostach, ré nua d'airm ionsaithe   23

Spicy Honey Chicken (with Broccoli)   24
Sicín Milis Spíosrach (le Brocailí)   25

In Decay, Great Britain — but Still Beautiful   26
Tá an Bhreatain Mhór go hálainn. ach is ag meath atá sí freisin   27

Chicken Alfredo   28
Sicín Alfredo   30

English Language Changed by Hip-Hop Forever   32
An Béarla athraithe go deo ag an hip-hap   33

Albariño – Is it the Next Great White Wine?	34
An é an chéad mhórfhíon geal eile é Albariño?	35
Convicts in Russian Army say, 'We Are Not Human to Them'	36
'Ní daoine sinn dar leo': saol na gcimí in arm na Rúise	37
American Hot Dogs – A Field Guide	38
Treoirleabhar allamuigh do mhórbhrocairí teo Mheiriceá	39
Neighbour Dead – Rats all About the Empty House – Help!	40
Cailleadh comharsa léi – tá francaigh ag síolrú anois sa teach folamh; cad is ceart di a dhéanamh?	41
Werner Herzog Lands New Job in AI	42
Ról nua do Werner Herzog in I.S.	43
Addiction Treatment Eludes More Than Half of Americans in Need	44
Seachnaíonn Cóir Leighis Breis is Leath de na Meiriceánaigh atá ina Gátar	45
Tony Blair – He's back!	46
Tony Blair ar ais	47
Chitty Chitty Bang Bang's Famous Windmill is up for Sale if you have the Sterling…	48
Muileann gaoithe a thuill clú in 'Chitty Chitty Bang Bang' ar díol i Sasana…	49
Nights on Mars Getting Longer	50
Laethanta ar Mhars ag dul i nGiorracht	51
What Next for Last Survivors of Amazonian Tribe Found in Brazil	52
Tháinig an Bhrasaíl ar an mbeirt dheireanach de threibh Amasónach. agus anois?..	53

Plans to Drop Languages at West Virginia University as
Part of Belt Tightening Measures   54
*Ollscoil West Virginia chun an buiséad a ghearradh go mór
agus beartaithe aici éirí as teangacha*   55

A Cleverer Way to Give your Plants a Watering   56
Slí níos cliste chun do chuid plandaí a uisciú   57

The Political Spokesperson of Native American Voices,
Ada Deer, Dies Aged 88…   58
*Ada Deer ar lár in aois 88, guth na nDúchasach
Meiriceánach laistigh agus lasmuigh den rialtas…*   59

Climate Change Stresses Damselfish as
Warming Seas Affect their Brains   60
*Bé-éisc suaite: d'fhéadfadh farraigí níos teolaí
mearbhall a chur orthu*   61

Masses of African Migrants Allegedly
Killed by Saudi Border Guards   62
*Marú na gCéadta imirceach Afracach curtha
i leith ghardaí teorann de chuid na hAraibe Sádaí*   63

Clearly, Ron DeSantis is on a Downward Slide as
He is overtaken by Another   64
*Is léir nach bhfuil dul chun cinn á dhéanamh a
thuilleadh ag ron DeSantis, ach tá ag duine éigin eile*   65

From the Shadows, he Trails the Difficult to
Find Amazon Tribes   66
*É sa tóir ar threibheanna éalaitheacha san Amasónacha,
ach faoi choim*   67

Russian TV Sells Military Service as Enhancing
Manliness, Reputation and Lucrative   68
*Fearúlacht, gradam agus airgead tirim: an
tSlí a nDíoltar seirbhís mhíleata ar theilifís na Rúise*   69

16-Foot Trump Tower Clock Which No One Knew About	70
An raibh a fhios agat faoin gClog 16 troithe	
ar Thúr Trump? ní raibh a fhios ag an gcathair ach oiread	72
History Education in Texas – How it Appears	74
An chuma atá ar mhúineadh na staire in Texas	75
Trump Swears he Staved off 'Nuclear Catastrophe'	76
Deir Trump agus é faoi mhionn gur sheachain	
sé 'uileloscadh núicléach'	77
Feelings of Oblivion by Those Worn Out by War	
and Earthquakes	78
In áit atá scriosta ag cogadh is ag creathanna talún,	
braitheann daoine go bhfuil siad ligthe i ndearmad	79
Iarfhocal (Saghas)/ Afterword (Of Sorts)	80
Appendix (1)	94
Appendix (2)	95
Appendix (3)	97
Poetry Titles from Gabriel Rosenstock	98
About the Author	*100*
About Revival Press	*101*

Miami and the Rising Seas

Miami can go f**k itself,
or is it 'herself'?
Masculine, feminine, neuter –
or something else?

Miami comes from a native word
myaamiwa, meaning "a downstream person".
Who would have guessed?

Deir Miami go mBeidh sé in ann Déileáil le hArdú na bhFarraigí

Féadann sé é féin a scriúáil
nó í féin? Firinscneach, baininscneach
nó neodrach? Nó rud éigin eile?

Tagann sé ón bhfocal *myaamiwa,* a chiallaíonn
"duine ó cheantar bhéal na habhann".
Cé a shamhlódh é?

Legal Bills and Trump Cash Crunch

No need to worry, my friend.
I've been down to my local church
here in Sallynoggin
and raided the poor box.
Money is winging its way to you now.
Your mother was a native speaker of Gaelic.
You can't be all bad.

Billí dlíodóirí ag ardú agus Trump i sáinn ó Thaobh airgead reatha de

Ná bí buartha, a chara.
Bhuaileas síos go dtí an séipéal áitiúil
anseo sa Naigín
agus dheineas creach ar bhosca na mbocht.
Tá pinginí ar a slí chugat.
Bhí Gaeilge na hAlban ag do mháthairse ón gcliabhán.
Ní fhéadfadh gur lofa go smior atá tú.

Fund to Vacuum Greenhouse Gases

Throw money at it. It's the only way. Right?
Just, be careful with the stars! OK?
We don't want them sucked away.
Remember Oscar Wilde:
"We are all in the gutter
but some of us are looking at the stars."

Caithfidh SAM $1.2 billiún chun gás ceaptha teasa a fholúsghlanadh den spéir

Caithigí airgead leis. Níl aon bhealach eile ann. Ceart?
Ach bígí cúramach leis na réaltaí. Le bhur dtoil?
Ní mian linn go súfaí as an spéir iad.
Cuimhnígí ar Oscar Wilde:
"Sa lathach atáimid go léir
ach tá cuid againn ag breathnú ar na réaltaí."

Wagner Group, Ready for Coup

Well, I hope so! I'm planning a coup in Ireland and I sure could do with some help here, guys. First, we'll take Dublin, then Cork and Belfast.

- ------ ----------
"*(@$"! Hello? Mayo calling!
(Crackle on the line)
Hello? +-)&^%£. Hello? Don't forget Mayo!"

An Grupa Wagner reidh i gcónaí le haghaidh coup

Tá súil le Dia agam go bhfuil! Tá coup á phleanáil agamsa anseo in Éirinn agus tá cabhair de dhíth orm, a leaideanna.

Bleá Cliath ar dtús, ansin Corcaigh is Béal Feirste.

- - - - - - - - - - - - - - - -
"*(@$"! Hóra hóra! Maigh Eo ag glaoch.
(Brioscarnach ar an líne)
Heileo? +-)&^%£. Hóra hóra! Ná dearmad Maigh Eo!"

First Russian Spacecraft for Fifty Years Headed to the Moon

I have some advice for you.
Be on your guard.
There's a gigantic vacuum-cleaning job in progress.
It cost $1.2 billion, so it's got to be good. Right?
A cosmic blow job – the most fantastic thing ever.
So, watch out!

Den chéad uair le leathchéad bliain anuas nach mór, tá spásárthach lainseáilte ag an Rúis agus í ag triall ar an nGealach

Glacaigí le mo chomhairlese.
Bígí san airdeall.
Tá jab ollmhór folúsghlantóireachta ar siúl.
£1.2 billiún a chosain sé, mar sin caithfidh
go bhfuil fiúntas leis. Ceart? Séideog chosmach –
an rud is iontaí riamh.
Mar sin, seachnaígí!

Hawaii to Reinvent Itself after 2023 Wildfires

Now all that is left to do is to chant, for strength:

    E iho ana a luna

    E pi'i ana o lalo

    E hui ana na moku

    E ku ana ka paia

Tar éis an uafáis is an dobróin, athróidh Háváí í féin ó bhonn

Níl le déanamh anois ach neart a lorg sa chantaireacht :

    E iho ana a luna

    E pi'i ana o lalo

    E hui ana na moku

    E ku ana ka paia

A New Era of Inexpensive Add-On Assault Weapons Spawned

From his resting place
in Saint Matthew's Episcopal Church
Pacific Palisades, Los Angeles,
Charlton Heston whispers
in his best Ben-Hur accent
Deo gratias . . .

Breiseán neamhchostach, ré nua d'airm ionsaithe

Ón seanbhaile aige
in Eaglais Easpagóideach Naomh Matha
Pacific Palisades, Cathair na nAingeal,
arsa Charlton Heston i gcogar –
ní fhéadfadh Bein Húr é a rá níos fearr –
Deo gratias . . .

Spicy Honey Chicken (with Broccoli)*

When first it began to run around
in China
6,000 years before Christ
did it ever imagine it might end up
as spicy honey chicken
in a recipe in the *New York Times?*

---

* See also:
An Chearc/ The Hen by Gabriel Rosenstock,
illustrated by Masood Hussain.
(Published by Lulu, ISBN 9781447895992)

Sicín milis spíosrach (le brocailí)

Nuair a thosaigh sé ag rith thart ar dtús
Sa tSín
6,000 bliain roimh Chríost
Ar shamhlaigh sé riamh gurbh é a bhí i ndán dó
Ná bheith ina shicín milis spíosrach
in oideas sa *New York Times?*

In Decay, Great Britain – but Still Beautiful

Tell us something we don't know:
what it's like to see the whites of their eyes –
lifers

Tell us about the silence on the branch –
the broken branch

Everything is decaying

My much-loved cousin Brendan Langlois-Kennedy
moved into a housing estate 'for decayed gentry'
and then he died;
the estate was built in 1761 in Co. Cork
by James, Fourth Lord Baron Kingston –
up to his tonsils in Freemasonry –
he's dead too

Tá an Bhreatain Mhór go hÁlainn – ach is ag meath atá sí freisin

Abair rud éigin nach bhfuil ar eolas againn:
conas a bhraitheann sé féachaint i súile na gcimí úd
ar gearradh príosún saoil orthu

Inis dúinn faoi chiúnas na géige –
an ghéag bhriste

Tá an uile ní ag meath
Bhog col ceathrair ionúin liom, Breandan Langlois-Kennedy,

isteach in eastát tithíochta d'uaislibh a bhí ag meath
agus cailleadh é;
James, an Ceathrú Barún Kingston
(báite sa mháisiúnachas a bhí sé)
a thóg an t-eastát sa bhliain 1761 –
tá seisean leis ar shlí na fírinne

Chicken Alfredo

Another recipe from the New York Times.
Not as depressing
as the god-damn awful news.
Who was this Alfredo person?
Anybody know?
Anybody care?
Just eat the damn chicken
chew
digest
defecate
that's it?
And Alfredo?
Who he, pray?
Alfredo di Lelio created Chicken Alfredo
in 1914, in Rome.
That's Rome, Italy,
not Rome New York
Rome Illinois
Rome Indiana
Rome Kentucky
or any other damned Rome.
How many more Romes are there?
Looks like all roads lead to Rome . . .
Rome Georgia
Rome Maine
Rome Mississippi
Rome Missouri
Rome Ohio
Rome Oregon
Rome Pennsylvania
Rome Tennessee
hey, give me a break.
While others were busy
with the First World War (1914-1918)
Alfredo was busy making Chicken Alfredo.
Alfredo di Lelio, master chef, should not be confused

With Alfredo di Lelio, minor poet (1880-1914).
Alfredo di Lelio, minor poet, published only one book,
or so it is said,
but no copy remains
so, we can't say for certain was he major or minor.
Furthermore, his book was written in dialect.
The beginning of *The Lord's Prayer* in Italian:
> *Padre nostro, che sei nei cieli,*
> *sia santificato il tuo nome . . .*

In Alfredo the Poet's dialect:
> *Attàne Nèste, ca sta 'ngile,*
> *sandificàte jè u nome tuje . . .*

What chance did he have, in Rome, Rome Italy?
Rome New York
Rome Illinois
Rome Indiana
Rome Kentucky etc.
Forget it.
Alfredo the Poet was not one of the 460,000 Italians (approx.)
slaughtered in the First World War.
Cause of death: choked on a chicken bone.
Not Chicken Alfredo, however,
as it would be six weeks and two days
before the other Alfredo
came up with Chicken Alfredo.

Sicín Alfredo

Oideas eile ón *New York Times*
nach bhféachann chomh hainnis in aon chor
leis an nuacht mhallaithe seo go léir.
Cérbh é mo dhuine, Alfredo?
An bhfuil a fhios ag éinne?
An cás le héinne é mar scéal?
Ith an sicín damnaithe
cogain
díleaigh
cac
an é sin é?
Agus Alfredo?
Cérbh é féin?
Ba é Alfredo di Lelio a chruthaigh Sicín Alfredo
Sa bhliain 1914, sa Róimh,
Róimh na hIodáile,
Seachas Róimh Nua-Eabhrac
An Róimh Illinois
An Róimh Indiana
An Róimh Kentucky
Nó Róimh ar bith eile, damnú orthu go léir.
An mó Róimh eile atá ann?
Tá aghaidh gach bóthair ar an Róimh, is cosúil . . .
An Róimh Georgia
An Róimh Maine
An Róimh Mississippi
An Róimh Missouri
An Róimh Ohio
An Róimh Oregon
An Róimh Pennsylvania
An Róimh Tennessee
hé, tabhair sos dom.
Nuair a bhí daoine eile gafa
leis an gCéad Chogadh Domhanda (1914-1918)
gafa le Sicín Alfredo a bhí Alfredo.
Ná meascar an dá Alfredo, an cócaire

agus Alfredo di Lelio, mionfhile (1880-1914).
Níor fhoilsigh Alfredo di Lelio, file, ach leabhar amháin,
nó sin a deirtear, i gcanúint aisteach.
Níl aon chóip fágtha
mar sin cá bhfios an mórfhile nó mionfhile a bhí ann.
Tús an *Ár nAthair* san Iodáilis:
> *Padre nostro, che sei nei cieli,*
> *sia santificato il tuo nome . . .*

I gcanúint Alfredo, file:
> *Attàne Nèste, ca sta 'ngile,*
> *sandificàte jè u nome tuje . . .*

Cén seans a bhí aige sa Róimh, Róimh na hIodáile,
Róimh Nua-Eabhrac
An Róimh Illinois
An Róimh Indiana
An Róimh Kentucky etc.
Déan dearmad air.

Níor dhuine de na 460,000 Iodálach (go garbh) é
Alfredo file a cailleadh in ár an Chéad Chogadh Domhanda.
Cnámh sicín a ghreamaigh ina scornach ba thrúig bháis dó.
Ní Sicín Alfredo a bhí ann
mar bheadh sé seachtaine agus dhá lá ann
sula gcruthódh an Alfredo eile
Sicín Alfredo.

English Language Changed by Hip-Hop Forever

English English English English
Why is it always about English?
English English English English . . .
Enough already
Genug schoyn!

Read how B. Traven attempted to replace English with Nahuatl, the language of the Aztecs, in the sensational book *Sherlock Holmes agus an Smig Bhréige*. (Lulu, ISBN 9781312583528) in which the sleuth and his lapdog Dr Watson are hot on the anarchist's trail, the famous duo well aware that the English language is the very cornerstone of the stability of Empire.

An Béarla athraithe go deo ag an hip-hap

Béarla Béarla Béarla Béarla
Cén fáth Béarla an t-am go léir?
Béarla Béarla Béarla Béarla . . .
Is leor sin
Genug schoyn!

Albariño – Is it the Next Great White Wine?

Couldn't care less.
I only *drink* red.
Note the emphasis on *drink*.
I drink the stuff.
I don't read about it.
Similarly with food.
Eat it, for God's sake.
Stop reading about it.
Stop talking about it.
All those words about wine.
Instead of learning the language of wine
why not go out and do something to save a dying language?
Attack: When a wine says, 'Sit up! Pay attention!'
Bad eggs: Badly-cellared wine will stink.
It goes on and on:
Cat's Pee, Clumsy, Hollow,
Old Socks, Flabby.
It's all a bit much, no?
Each to his own, I suppose.

An é an chéad mhórfhíon geal eile é Albariño?

Is cuma sa sioc.
Ní *ólaimse* ach fíon dearg.
Béim ar an *ól*.
Ólaimse é.
Ní léimse ina thaobh.
An rud céanna i gcás bia.
I gcuntas Dé, ith é.
Stop ag léamh mar gheall air.
Stop ag caint ina thaobh.
An friotal go léir a bhaineann le fíon.
In áit friotal an fhíona a fhoghlaim
cad faoi rud éigin a dhéanamh faoi theanga atá i bponc?
Ionsaí: Fíon a deir, 'Suigh suas go díreach! Tabhair aire!'
Uibheacha lofa: Beidh drochbholadh uaidh
        mura gcoinnítear i gceart sa siléar é.
Agus mar sin de ar aghaidh is ar aghaidh:
Mún Cait, Amscaí, Folamh,
Seanstocaí, Séidte.
Beagáinín iomarcach, nach bhfuil?
Gach mac mar a oiltear is an lacha ar an uisce.

Convicts in Russian Army say, 'We Are Not Human to Them'

There are no humans left in prisons
No humans left in restaurants
No humans left in offices
No humans left in parking lots
No humans left in factories
No humans left in shopping malls
No humans left in newspaper offices
No humans left in universities
No humans left in hospitals
No humans left in publishing houses
No humans left in gated communities
No humans left in slums
No humans left in churches
No humans left in cars
No humans left in aeroplanes
No humans left in telephone booths
No humans left in government buildings
No humans left among the refugees
No humans left in armies
No humans left in graveyards
No humans anywhere

'Ní daoine sinn dar leo': saol na gcimí in arm na Rúise

Níl daoine ar bith fágtha i gcarcair
Níl daoine fágtha i mbialanna
Níl daoine fágtha in oifigí
Níl daoine fágtha i gcarrchlóis
Níl daoine fágtha i monarchana
Níl daoine fágtha in ionaid shiopadóireachta
Níl daoine fágtha in oifigí nuachtán
Níl daoine fágtha in ollscoileanna
Níl daoine fágtha in ospidéil
Níl daoine fágtha i dtithe foilsitheoireachta
Níl daoine fágtha i bpobail gheataithe
Níl daoine fágtha i slumaí
Níl daoine fágtha i dteampaill
Níl daoine fágtha i ngluaisteáin
Níl daoine fágtha in eitleáin
Níl daoine fágtha i mboscaí gutháin
Níl daoine fágtha i dtithe an rialtais
Níl daoine fágtha i measc na dteifeach
Níl daoine fágtha in airm
Níl daoine fágtha i reiligí
Níl daoine fágtha aon áit.

American Hot Dogs – A Field Guide

?

Treoirleabhar allamuigh do mhórbhrocairí teo Mheiriceá

?

Neighbour Dead – Rats all About the Empty House – Help!

Madam, you must go to the Karni Mata temple
in India. Immediately.
There are 20,000 rats there.
They'll scurry across the temple floor to meet you
sit in your lap and allow you to pet them.
Offer them *prasad* – food – such as coconut,
grain. Sugar.
They wouldn't say no to a drop of liquor.
Nibble some food which they have nibbled on –
it's finger-lickin' good. I promise.
One drop of their saliva is recommended
for whatever might be ailing you
such as musophobia. Fear of rats.
But, Madam, be careful.
If you accidentally step on a rat –
if your fashionable high heel pierces its body –
so that it writhes there in front of you
its saintly eyes popping out of its head
you must replace the rat immediately
with one made of pure gold or silver.

Cailleadh comharsa léi – tá francaigh ag síolrú anois sa teach folamh – cad is ceart di a dhéanamh?

A bhean mhaith, beidh ort dul chuig teampall
Karni Mata, san India. Ar an toirt.
Tá 20,000 francach ann.
Scinnfidh siad chugat chun fáilte a chur romhat.
Suífidh siad id' bhaclainn is ligfidh duit
peataireacht a dhéanamh orthu.
Ofráil *prasad* dóibh – bia – cnó cócó, abair,
grán. Siúcra.
Ní dhiúltóidís don bhraon cruaidh.
Blais de bhia atá creimthe acusan –
déanfaidh sé maitheas duit. Geallaimse duit.
Leigheas ar gach aon rud is ea braon dá gcuid seile,
eagla roimh fhrancaigh cuirem i gcás.
Ach bí cúramach, a bhean mhaith.
Dá satlófá trí thimpiste (ar ndóigh) ar fhrancach –
sáil ard ghalánta leat á tholladh
é ag lúbarnaíl ar nós an diabhail os do chomhair
na súile beannaithe ag at ina cheann,
bheadh ort francach eile a chur ina áit
francach airgid nó francach d'ór buí.

Werner Herzog Lands New Job in AI

Mein Gott, Werner, was hast du gemacht? Mensch!
Narrating 87 poems written by an AI bot!
You don't even have a mobile phone . . .
The critics say that the poems express a longing
to connect with humanity. You betcha!

Ról nua do Werner Herzog in I.S.

Mein Gott, Werner, was hast du gemacht? Mensch!
87 ndán a chum bota I.S. á n-aithris agat!
Níl fón póca agat fiú amháin . . .
Deir na criticeoirí go léiríonn na dánta gur mian leo
teagmháil a dhéanamh leis an gcine daonna. Déarfainn é!

Addiction Treatment Eludes More Than Half of Americans in Need

Now that's an odd word to use, 'eludes'!
The situation isn't funny, I know,
but it's hard not to imagine the eluders:
'Quick! Down this lane! They'll never find us!
Heads down, everyone!
Shit! Game's up!
Who are you? What do you want?'

'I'm looking for the wrinkles
on Mahākāśyapa's face . . .'   *

---

* YouTube: 30 min. of Pure Genius – Alan Watts on *The Gateless Gate*

Seachnaíonn Cóir Leighis Breis is Leath de na Meiriceánaigh atá ina Gátar

Is aisteach an focal é, 'seachain'.
Tuigim nach scéal greannmhar é seo
ach is deacair gan na seachantóirí a shamhlú:
'Seo linn síos an lána seo go beo! Ní thiocfar orainn ann!
Cloigne síos, gach éinne!
Cac an diabhail air! Táimid aimsithe acu!
Cé thú féin? Cad atá uait?'

'Táim ag lorg na roc
ar chuntanós Mahākāśyapa's . . .'

Tony Blair – He's back!

          Why?
Why do they have to return?
Return of the Vampire
Return of the Jedi
Return of the Dragon
Return of the Pink Panther
Return of the Joker
Return of the King
Return of Xander Cage
Return of the Living Dead
Return of Swamp Thing
Return of the Killer Tomatoes
Return of Mr Moto
Return of the One-Armed Swordsman
Return of Count Yorga
And now . . .
The Return of Tony Blair!

Tony Blair ar ais

                    Cén fáth?
Cén fáth a dtagann siad ar ais?
An Súmaire ar ais
An Jeidí ar ais
An Dragan ar ais
An Pantar Bándearg ar ais
Fear na gCrúb ar ais
An Rí ar ais
Xander Cage ar ais
Na Mairbh Bheo ar ais
An Rud as an gCorcach ar ais
Na Trátaí Marfacha ar ais
An tUasal Mótó ar ais
Claimhteoir na Leathláimhe ar ais
An Cunta Yorga ar ais
Agus anois . . .
Tony Blair ar ais!

Chitty Chitty Bang Bang's Famous Windmill is up for Sale if you have the Sterling

I'm not going to put up with it anymore
No way
I've reached the end of my patience
This is a mockery
I've had enough
No wonder they call me
The knight of the sad figure.
Come on now, Rocinante, shake a leg
We have important work to do!

Muileann gaoithe a thuill clú in 'Chitty Chitty Bang Bang' ar díol i Sasana

Nílimse chun cur suas leis níos mó
Nílim ambaiste
Bhris ar an bhfoighne orm fadó
Táthar ag magadh fúinn
An aon ionadh go dtugann siad
Caballero de triste figura orm
Seo leat anois, a Rocinante, cuir cruth ort féin
Tá obair thábhachtach le déanamh againn!

Nights on Mars Getting Longer

As if we hadn't enough to worry about.
But let me tell you . . .
The ruling class (and the media they own)
want to keep us worried
about every damn thing.
Every day a new worry.
And if they can't think of a worrisome thing
they'll bloody well invent it.
(And throw in a recipe for Chicken Alfredo
just so we don't go completely off the rails).
No one has time to read every story
but headlines sink in
and begin to fester in the brain.
I don't know what's behind the Mars story.
Will it win a Pulitzer?
Guess what, Joseph Pulitzer himself
was a master of fake news and yellow journalism.

Laethanta ar Mhars ag dul i nGiorracht

Nach bhfuil ábhar imní ár ndóthain againn.
Ach éist . . .
Is mian leis an aicme cheannais (agus a gcuid meán)
go mbeimis buartha
faoi gach aon ní.
Imní nua in aghaidh an lae.
Munar féidir leo smaoineamh ar údar imní
cumfaidh siad scéal éigin.
(Tabharfaidh siad oideas le haghaidh Sicín Alfredo dúinn
Chun nach raghaimis le gealaigh ar fad).
Níl am ag éinne chun gach diabhal scéal a léamh
ach téann ceannlínte i bhfeidhmn orainn
agus tosaíonn ag ábhrú istigh ionainn.
N'fheadarsa cad atá laistiar de scéal Mhars.
An ngnóthóidh sé Duais Pulitzer?
An gcreidfeá é – máistir ar nuacht bhréige
agus ar an iriseoireacht lathaí
ab ea Joseph Pulitzer féin.

What Next for Last Survivors of Amazonian Tribe Found in Brazil?

In 1981, one of the original INNTI poets
whom I counted as a friend – Liam Ó Muirthile –
interviewed the last native speakers of Irish
in the Burren of Co. Clare.
One of them was Mairéad Ní Uallaigh
her name Anglicised in a Ginsbergian fashion
to Maggie Howley
and as it was a TV interview
Liam had to keep his howl well locked up inside him
when he learned she had no running water
and no electricity

Tháinig an Bhrasaíl ar an mbeirt dheireanach de threibh Amasónach – agus anois?

Duine d'fhilí INNTI
agus cara liom – Liam Ó Muirthile –
chuir sé agallamh sa bhliain 1981
ar chainteoirí Gaeilge deireanacha
Bhoireann an Chláir.
Duine acu ab ea Mairéad Ní Uallaigh
nó Maggie Howley sa tSacs-Bhéarla
ainm a mheabhródh Ginsberg duit
ach ós agallamh teilifíse a bhí ann
b'éigean do Liam a ruabhéic a chosc
ar chloisint dó nach raibh uisce reatha aici
ná leictreachas.

Plans to Drop Languages at West Virginia University as Part of Belt Tightening Measures

And make way for other studies
forensics
engineering
neuroscience

Ollscoil West Virginia chun an buiséad a ghearradh go mór agus beartaithe aici éirí as teangacha

Agus slí a dhéanamh d'ábhair eile
an fhóiréinsic
an innealtóireacht
an néareolaíocht

A Cleverer Way to Give your Plants a Watering

A smarter way to do this
To do that
They're always at it!
Coming up with smarter ways . . .
Smarty Pants!
Implicit in the Smarter Way School of Marketing
Is that we were all stupid up to now.
Complete assholes!
Ah! But *now* we know – now we have the smarter way.
Maybe I should get into this smarter-way business.
A smarter way to get out of bed.
A smarter way to pee.
A smarter way to gargle.
A smarter way to gargle your pee.
A smarter way to eat Chicken Alfredo.
A smarter way to win the war in Ukraine.
A smarter way to manipulate people
And laugh all the way to the bank.
A smarter way to read *The New York Times*.

Slí níos cliste chun do chuid plandaí a uisciú

Slí níos cliste chun seo
Nó siúd a dhéanamh.
Bíonn siad ag gabháilt dó de shíor!
Ag cumadh slite nua chun . . .
Saoithíní!
Tá sé le tuiscint ó Scoil Mhargaíochta an Bhealaigh Chliste
Gur dúr a bhíomar go léir go dtí seo.
Clasáin chearta!
Ach tá's againn anois – is eol dúinn slí níos cliste.
N'fheadar an ceart dom dul leis an ngnó níos cliste seo.
Slí níos cliste chun éirí as an leaba.
Slí níos cliste chun do mhún a dhéanamh.
Slí níos cliste chun craosfholcadh a dhéanamh.
Slí níos cliste chun do mhún a chraosfholcadh.
Slí níos cliste chun Sicín Alfredo a ithe.
Slí níos cliste chun an bua a fháil san Úcráin.
Slí níos cliste chun dul i gcion ar dhaoine
Agus gáire a dhéanamh an tslí ar fad go dtí an banc.
Slí níos cliste chun an *New York Times* a léamh.

The Political Spokesperson of Native American Voices, Ada Deer, Dies Aged 88

You belonged to the Menominee tribe.
According to folklore you've always been there
for you belonged to the Ancient Ones
the *Kiash Matchitiwuk*
older than trees – but their equal
upright like them, strong,
peaceful and trustworthy

When your people looked into
a river or lake
it was an honest face they saw.

Ada Deer ar lár in aois 88, guth na nDúchasach Meiriceánach laistigh agus lasmuigh den rialtas

Ba leis an treibh Menominee thú.
De réir an bhéaloidis, bhíomhair riamh ann
mar gur bhaineamhair leis an bPobal Ársa
na *Kiash Matchitiwuk*
níos sine ná na crainn – ach ar comhstádas leo,
a ndála féin, ionraic, téagartha,
síochánta agus iontaofa

Má chromamhair os cionn abhann
nó locha
aghaidh mhacánta a d'fhéach ar ais oraibh

Climate Change Stresses Damselfish as Warming Seas Affect their Brains

Damselfish?
It's not just me, then?

Bé-éisc suaite: d'fhéadfadh farraigí níos teolaí mearbhall a chur orthu

Bé-éisc?
Ní mise amháin é mar sin?

Masses of African Migrants Allegedly Killed by Saudi Border Guards

Though roughly 750,000 Ethiopians live
and work in Saudi Arabia
those who cross into the country from Yemen
are regularly shot at.
One boy who managed to escape said:
"Bullets fell like rain!"

Marú na gcéadta imirceach Afracach curtha i leith ghardaí teorann de chuid na hAraibe Sádaí

Bíodh is go bhfuil 750,00 Aetópach (go garbh)
ag cur fúthu is ag obair san Araib Shádach
scaoiltear urchair go rialta leo siúd
a thagann isteach sa tír ó Éimin.
Arsa leaidín ar éirigh leis na cosa a thabhairt leis:
"Ag teacht ina gcith a bhí na piléir!"

Clearly, Ron DeSantis is on a Downward Slide as He is overtaken by Another

Who? Who!
That's another sneaky headline from the *NYT*.
Who's on the rise?
I'm being sucked into this story
Like all the other dumb stories
That I never wanted to read in the first place.
Surely there are creatures much more interesting
To read about than these two dummies – such as
Let me think . . .
The Akond of Swat!

      WHO, or why, or which, or what,
          Is the Akond of Swat?
      Is he tall or short, or dark or fair?
  Does he sit on a stool or a sofa or chair,
           OR SQUAT?
         The Akond of Swat?

Is léir nach bhfuil dul chun cinn á dhéanamh a thuilleadh ag Ron deSantis, ach tá ag duine éigin eile

Cé? Cé!
Ceannlíne shleamhain eile ón NYT.
Cé atá ag déanamh dul chun cinn?
Táim súite isteach sa scéal seo
Ar nós na scéalta amaideacha eile go léir
Scéalta nár theastaigh uaim a léamh sa chéad áit.
Caithfidh go bhfuil neacha níos spéisiúla ann
Ná an dá ghamal seo – ar nós
Lig dom smaoineamh . . .

     An Cunta de Svat!
   CÉ, nó canathaobh nó cad é? Fut fat!
    Ciacu eisean, an Cunta de Svat?
    An fathach atá ann nó leipreachán
   An mbuaileann sé gach maidin a thóinín bán
       LE SLAT?
     An Cunta de Svat!

From the Shadows, he Tracks the Difficult to Find Amazon Tribes

Who are we talking about here?
Who is this tracker?
Headlines have fried my brain.
Is it DeSantis?
The Akond of Swot? There's a thought.
Alfredo di Lelio?
Dead.
Roberto Bolaño? Dead.
Werner Herzog?
Unlikely.
Trump?
Isn't he in jail?
Tony Blair?
Isn't he in jail?
Come out, come out whoever you are!

É sa tóir ar threibheanna éalaitheacha san Amasóin, ach faoi choim

Cé air a bhfuilimid ag caint?
Cé hé an lorgaire seo?
Tá m'inchinn friochta ag ceannlínte.
An é DeSantis é?
An Cunta de Svat? Sin smaoineamh.
Alfredo di Lelio?
Marbh.
Roberto Bolaño? Marbh.
Werner Herzog?
Drochsheans.
Trump?
Nach i bpríosún atá sé siúd?
Tony Blair?
Nach i bpríosún atá sé siúd?
Amach leat, amach, cibé thú féinig!

Russian TV Sells Military Service as Enhancing Manliness, Reputation and Lucrative

What about the grub?
I hear they serve Chicken Alfredo on Sundays!

Fearúlacht, gradam agus airgead tirim: an tslí a ndíoltar seirbhís mhíleata ar theilifís na Rúise

Cad faoin mbia?
Cloisim go mbíonn Sicín Alfredo acu ar an Domhnach!

16-Foot Trump Tower Clock Which No One Knew About

Thank you for the headline!
It made me want to read
George Woodcock's pamphlet again
The Tyranny of the Clock
Where he reminds us of the ways
We once represented time
By the cyclic process of nature:
Day following night
Season following season

The nomad and the farmer
Measuring their day
From sunrise to sunset.
Measuring the year
From seedtime to harvest

A falling leaf
Ice thawing on lakes and rivers.

Deadlines?
The craftsman toiled until
With a sigh of pleasure
He looked at his work
And said, 'Finished!'

Industrial capitalism came along
And everything became subject to the clock.
Even young lovers in Dublin arranged to meet
'Under Clerys clock.'
Woodcock says that men became clocks:
'Regular as clockwork.'

Those who – after a long day –
Sought refuge in an ale-house
Their stories and ballads were interrupted
By those deadly words
Deadlier than anything
In Bolaño's *The Savage Detectives*:
'Time, gentlemen, please!'

In Tigh Daniel
A pub in Kerry
There was a clock that went backwards.
It was a favourite haunt of the INNTI poets
Where Seán de hÓra used to sing *
'Tá bó agam ar an sliabh'
(*I have a cow on the moor*).
We knew then, if only for a second,
That we had vanquished Time.

---

* *Seán de Hóra: Bean Dubh an Ghleanna (YouTube)*

An raibh a fhios agat faoin gclog 16 troithe ar Thúr Trump? ní raibh a fhios ag an gcathair ach oiread

Go raibh maith agaibh as an gceannlíne sin!
Bhí fonn orm paimfléad
De chuid George Woodcock a léamh arís
Tíorántacht an Chloig
Ina meabhraítear dúinn na slite
A gcuirtí an t-am in iúl
Trí phróiseas timthriallach an nádúir:
Tar éis na hoíche an lá
Séasúir ag leanúint a chéile

An lá á thomhas
Ag an bhfánaí is ag an bhfeirmeoir
Ó éirí go luí na gréine.
An bhliain á tomhas
Ó am curtha an tsíl go dtí an fómhar

Titim na nduilleog
Oighear ag leá ar loch is ar abhainn

Sprioc-amanna?
D'oibrigh an ceardaí
Go dtí gur fhéach sé ar a shaothar
Gur lig osna phléisiúir
Is go ndúirt, 'Déanta!'

Tháinig an caipitleachas tionsclaíoch
Agus bheadh gach aon ní feasta ag freagairt don chlog.
Leannáin óga Bhleá Cliath fiú amháin
Casadh ar a chéile iad faoi Chlog Uí Chléirigh.
Deineadh clog den duine de réir Woodcock:
'Chomh rialta leis an gclog.'

Iad siúd – tar éis dóibh lá fada a chur díobh –
A lorg tearmann i dteach an óil
Cuireadh isteach ar a gcuid scéalta is ar a gcuid bailéad
Leis na focail uafásacha úd
Níos uafásasaí ná aon ní a gheofá
In *Los Detectives Salvajes* de chuid Bolaño
'Tá an t-am istigh, a fheara!'

I dTigh Daniel
Tábhairne i gCorca Dhuibhne
Bhí clog ann agus is siar a théadh sé.
B'aoibhinn le filí INNTI an áit.
Chanadh Seán de hÓra ann
'Tá bó agam ar an sliabh'
Agus bhí a fhios againn
Ar feadh soicind
Go raibh buaite againn ar an Am.

History Education in Texas – How it Appears

An chuma atá ar mhúineadh na staire in Texas

Trump Swears he Staved off 'Nuclear Catastrophe'

When Fernando Pessoa walked
Unannounced into the Pickwick Club
He felt at home.
Club member Mr Snodgrass, poet, offered him
A glass of port
Which reminded him of his home country, Portugal.
I find no home, no comfort
In these NYT headlines
On in headlines created closer to home.
Dr Pancrácio could do better!   *
Creators of headlines
Are the enemies of poetry!
Who can possibly contradict this?
No one who has read Pessoa.

In Richard Zenith's hypnotising biography, *Pessoa: An Experimental Life*, Richard Zenith informs us that Dr Pancrácio (Dr Know-Nothing) was a creator of poetry and riddles and a contributor to one of Pessoa's newspapers, written and produced by himself in early adolescence.

Deir trump agus é faoi mhionn gur sheachain sé 'uileloscadh núicléach'

Nuair a bhuail Fernando Pessoa isteach
Gan choinne go dtí an Pickwick Club
Bhraith sé ag baile.
Thairg ball den chlub, an tUasal Snodgrass, file,
Braon pórtfhíona dhó
A chuir a thír dhúchais, an Phortaingéil, i gcuimhne dhó.
Ní haon bhaile domsa ná ní sólás dom iad
Na ceannlínte seo ón *New York Times*
Ná ceannlínte níos cóngaraí don bhaile.
D'fhéadfadh an Dr Pancrácio jab níos fearr a dhéanamh.
Naimhde na héigse iad
Cruthaitheoirí na gceannlínte go léir!
Cé a d'fhéadfadh an ráiteas sin a bhréagnú
Má tá Pessoa léite aige.

Feelings of Oblivion by Those Worn Out by War and Earthquakes

Do Syrians think of al-Ma'arri
and follow the advice of their blind medieval poet?

> *Soften your tread.*
> *What is the earth's surface but bodies of the dead.*
> *Walk slowly in the air*
> *So you do not trample on the remains of God's servants.*

O, al-Ma'arri, sightless poet,
are you still counting the bodies of the dead
in Aleppo and all over the Middle East?

In áit atá scriosta ag cogadh is ag creathanna talún, braitheann daoine go bhfuil siad ligthe i ndearmad

An smaoiníonn muintir na Siria ar al-Ma'arri?
An leanann siad comhairle an fhile gan radharc ón meánaois?

> *Siúil go réidh.*
> *Níl i ndromchla an domhain ach slua na marbh.*
> *Siúil go mall san aer*
> *Chun nach satlófá ar shearbhóntaí Dé*

A al-Ma'arri, a fhile atá dall,
an ag comhaireamh na marbh fós ataoi
ar shráideanna Aleppo is an Mheánoirthir go léir?

Iarfhocal (Saghas) /Afterword (Of Sorts)

I was asked recently by someone who had seen an infrarealistic poem of mine, "How do you reconcile your often ultra-refined poetry – ekphrastic tanka poems, in particular, which are frequently bhakti-flavoured, as well as your photo-haiku, many of which are ethereal and transcendental – how do you reconcile such exalted consciousness with what you call 'infraverse', something which is often downright vulgar, visceral and sensational?"

The only answer I could think of was this: I see myself as a devoted servant of the Irish language. I take her by the hand – she takes me by the hand? – and introduce her to places she has never seen, states of mind that she has not known, experiences that she has never had before, such as the 'infraverse', a word I've coined to describe both the poetry and the Weltanschauung of those, such as myself, who have imbibed tequila at the long, bare, dark counter of *Infrarrealismo*, or to give it its newly-coined name in Irish, *Infrearéalachas*. I introduce her to poets such as Syria's al-Ma'arri (973 – 1057). She has known many blind poets in the course of her long history. She has known exclusion, persecution.

Pessoa, the great Portuguese poet, had a hundred or so voices within him, some of them fairly dormant, and others erupting and saying their lines like characters out of a play he might have written. That's the way with me – and if I don't immediately recognise the voice that's coming from this new *infraverse*, it's because it is just one of many dormant voices in me that were long awaiting an awakening.

How does it work? It's simply a matter of channelling the spirit of *Infrarrealismo*, as one might channel one of its predecessors, Dada, founded by Tristan Tzara whose real name was Sami Rosenstock. It's not that Gabriel Rosenstock (me) is the result of one Big Bang and Sami Rosenstock (Tristan Tzara) the result of another. We're all connected in some way, and Pessoa gets a mention in my English-language comic detective novel, *My Head Is Missing* (Evertype 2016).

Mention is also made of Pessoa on page 90 of the controversial book *Sherlock Holmes agus an Smig Bhréige* (Lulu, 2023) in the context of a surreal incident involving former Finance Minister Pascal Donohue. In the same Sherlock Holmes book, we also come across the enigmatic B. Traven who attempts to replace English as a world language with Nahuatl. Dr Watson will have none of it! The Empire stands or falls on the strength and buoyancy of the English language.

The Irish-language, as tongue and Muse, is an ancient living stream whose destiny is unknown; she is incorruptible, because she renews herself hourly whenever she is employed in the telling of a good tale, or in a new form of poetry or song. She is self-cleansing, self-renewing, resurrected from the ashes.

Where will the next new form of poetry in Irish come from? When I co-founded the so-called INNTI movement and journal – a few years before the 20 odd poets in Mexico City got together to create *Infrarrealismo* – we didn't have a manifesto. Let's look now at sections of one of theirs, as translated by Timothy Pilcher:

> "Chirico says: thought needs to move away from everything called logic and common sense, to move away from all human obstacles in such a way that things take on a new look, as though illuminated by a constellation appearing for the first time. The infrarealists say: We're going to stick our noses into *all* human obstacles, in such a way that things begin to move *inside* of us, a hallucinatory vision of mankind . . ."

We are lacking in bold statements – whether intended to make much sense or not – 'we' meaning Irish-language poets. Had INNTI issued a campaign slogan, I'm afraid Brendan Behan's witticism would have applied immediately: the first item on the agenda of any Irish organisation is the split.

Nevertheless, new forms of poetry need new visions, as well as a brand-new engagement with the language, freed of its old containers and its traditional patrons and guardians. Not a language that hungers to be trendy, for there is nothing as fickle as fashion; a language that hungers to stay alive and be more alive than we currently conceive possible. Alive alive-o in unimpeded, impossible ways.

Infrarealists revolted against inertia, stultification and the double-faced smarminess of the bourgeoisie. What else could they do? Seek out the red carpet, fawningly, the champagne, the laurels, the works?

> 'These are hard times for poetry, some say, sipping tea, listening to music in their apartments, talking (listening) to the old masters. These are hard times for mankind, we say, coming back to the barricades after a workday full of shit and tear gas . . .'

Infras were stirring things up. Things always need a good stirring up.

Language needs stirring up. Poetry, above all, is duty bound to stir things up because its very nature revolts against stagnation, in society itself and in language.

A non-dualistic approach to the choices which life offers us (when it does) would be to have one's cake and eat it. So, if I have a lot of time for someone such as Roberto Bolaño from the *Infrarrealismo* camp – which I undoubtedly do – I would also have a lot of time for his bête noir, Octavio Paz, whom he plotted to kidnap!

Whether I like to admit it or not, my life's experience would have been closer to that of Paz. Streetwise, like Bolaño, I was not. But to say that this sudden attack of Infrarealism is nothing more than a very belated reaction to my own bourgeois upbringing is too easy an explanation. I don't buy it! I'm fascinated by *Infrearéalachas*, as another stone in my sling – aimed at nothingness, not merely as a self-correction process or to make up for years of fecklessness and neglect in terms of social awareness.

Now, was Paz, who wrote some wonderful haiku, all that different to Bolaño who was only 23 when he said "try to abandon everything everyday"? Bolaño's statement is very Zennish. So is this haiku by Paz. It's a bit too long. I shorten it in my transcreation:

Alzo los ojos: no hay nada.
Silencio sobre la rama
Sobre la rama quebrada

I raise my eyes: nothing
silence on the branch
broken branch

INNTI didn't have any money when we started off in University College, Cork. We had nothing but words, words to get off our chest, bardic words of ancient times mixed with mushroom-flavoured howls and whispers (Bob Dylan, Carlos Castaneda, Timothy Leary, Swami This & That, etc), words we foraged and never imagined they existed, such as *faoisceán*, which is a female crab. These kinds of creatures, as they fleshed out for us in what was for most of us an acquired, second language – albeit the senior language of our country – the hare, the wren, the mythical salmon, these were our *naguals*, the shape-shifting animal that was said to be present at the workshops and poetry readings of the Infras! We, too, were interested in myth and folklore, Celtic folklore, and the lore of animals, real and unreal.

To a greater or lesser degree, INNTI poets felt a tendency towards stridentism without ever having heard of Stridentism as a movement. Things float around, namelessly, in the ether, don't they, waiting for a language – any language – to give them shape and form. (For the record, *Estridentismo* was another precursor of *Infrarrealismo*, dating back to the 1920s.)

We weren't starving poets in a garret, but neither were we swanning around, chewing on Chicken Alfredo washed down by bottles of Albariño. Others dreamt of such things, students of dentistry and medicine, for instance. Educated in Ireland, many of them (when not extracting teeth or examining lumps) would quaff their Albariño in foreign fields, Dubai, Australia – wherever Nahuatl was not spoken.

Buying and selling of talent was anathema to the Infrarealists. I resigned, along with my co-editor at the time, Proinsias Ní Dhorchaí (1943 -1994), when after the sixth edition, money began to play an increasing role in INNTI's affairs. Grants, doled out of state coffers! The same state which was responsible for the shrinking of the Gaeltacht, the Irish-speaking areas devasted by emigration during the first fifty years and more of native government. The state that forgot about all the Maggie Howleys of this world.

What's wrong with money? That's the $64,000 question, isn't it? (I have tried to counteract the influence of buying and selling by offering some of my books for free. There's a sample list on my Wiki entry). But the world is structured to make it impossible not to be beholden to those who commodify everything. Capitalize on it! (Motto of CNBC).

I remember standing in the Quadrangle of University College Cork and as I wildly intoned INNTI! INNTI! like some fish-monger from a country I'd never heard of, crying SARDINES! SARDINES! FRESH FROM THE SEA! a gowned Professor of History scuttled past me and gave me a withering look.

Did I think to myself, 'INNTI poets will be famous one day and you'll regret you didn't buy a copy from me when you had a chance, you miserable *fualán!* (A *fualán* can mean a fool or a chamber-pot). But what would fame bring? One of the founders of the Infras, Rubén Medina, encapsulates their thinking:

"The Infrarealist poet hates becoming an official writer, the poet-winner of competitions, the writer with a job in an embassy, a bureaucratic writer (from the right or from the left), the one obsessed with his career and his place in the literary institution . . ."

The poem in this book for victims of the Hawaii wildfire cataclysm of August '23, the beginning of the brief period covered by these poems through the lenses of NYT headlines, incorporates a traditional chant. In the early days of INNTI, we were heading towards chant in many of our public performances, but never followed through. Some of today's poets, such as the mysterious Séamas Barra Ó Súilleabháin, take the rap route. Does something more indigenous than rap need to be discovered, or invented?

The people of Hawaii are victims of cultural colonisation and their disastrous fires in August 2023 bear witness to that. Ecological balance and cultural balance go hand-in-hand and with the disappearance of the native language came the introduction of non-native species of grasses that dried out quickly and the environment became less resistant to cataclysmic fires. (This is a study in itself which I'm not qualified to elaborate any further on).

The Infrarealists (they haven't gone away, you know) were capable of startling utterances. Many of us long for such utterances to appear in Irish, to spread as graffiti throughout the landscape, to soar as chant; to flower in barren, grey carparks, the sad sidewalls of empty churches, the polished lavatories of museums:

> "The true poet is the one who's always letting go of himself. Never too much time in the same place, like guerrillas, like UFOs, like the white eyes of prisoners serving life sentences."

That sounds like Bolaño, described by his fellow Chilean, Isabel Allende, as a "truly nasty person" – the price you may have to pay when you look into the eyes of lifers.

Creating poems around headlines from *The New York Times* seemed like an 'infra' thing to do. I knew nothing about the paper, except from what the perspicacious Caitlin Johnstone had to say about it in one of her copyright-free outpourings in prose and verse. She sounds to me like she may have read Bolaño:

> "I hate *The New York Times*. Hate it, hate it, hate it, hate it. With every fibre of my being, from the depths of my immortal soul.
>
> The 'paper of record' for the most murderous and tyrannical

nation on earth, *The New York Times* has been run by the same family since the late 1800s, during which time it has supported every depraved American war and has reliably dished out propaganda to manufacture consent for the political status quo necessary for the operation of a globe-spanning empire that is fuelled by human blood and suffering. It is a plague upon our world, and it should be destroyed, buried, and peed on."

Newspapers are powerful influencers, though their influence and their cash have been greatly reduced by competition from the digital world. Nevertheless, people are still investing in newspapers. A Japanese media firm bought *The Financial Times* for £844 million. They probably won't be employing Caitlin Johnstone! (Is she a Russian bot?)

The media could play a role in preventing wars and conflicts, if they had a mind to, collectively, but there's more money to be made out of war. We seem to be addicted to conflict. A *New York Times* headline on the 21st August 2023 – the month covered in this book – had a headline: *Even in War, Ukrainian Soldiers Find Time for World of Tanks Video Game*. That says a lot!

Peace Journalism, that wonderful and necessary concept proposed by Johan Galtung, needs to be taken very seriously. *The New York Times* is clearly not a platform for Peace Journalism; au contraire, it emphasises violence rather than looking at the whole picture, the underlying causes of conflict in terms of the culture and structure of societies that find themselves in bloody situations today. America's WASPish monolingualism is part of that Empire's problem. One of the headlines reproduced here referred to the University of Virginia's dropping languages in order to spend more time on such things as forensic science.

Every American university should offer courses in Conflict Studies and every American university should offer courses in Native American languages as well. Stanford offers courses in Hawaiian, Cherokee, Navajo, Yup'ik, Lakota, and Nahuatl. Bravo!

How about online courses in Native American languages, courtesy of *The New York Times*? One's thinking about life, society and the environment might benefit from such a course. What I like about Infrarrealismo is that it is not a product of WASP culture. In John Burdett's *The Godfather of Kathmandu* (Corgi 2010) we learn in his prefatory note that the heart chakra has shrunk to nothingness in the WASP! Check it out . . .

Peace journalism makes a lot of sense. Its ethical approach is "to allow opportunities for society at large to consider and value non-violent responses to conflict". Who in his right mind could see anything wrong with that?

Britain and the US were at loggerheads in 1859 because of a pig. The Pig War! I jest not. About fifty years later, Greece and Bulgaria started fighting when a Greek soldier ran after his dog, crossing the border into hostile territory. Britain went to war against Spain when a sailor by the name of Jenkins showed the English Parliament his rotten ear, severed by the Spaniards because of his smuggling activities. Let's declare war on those pesky Spaniards!

There's more! Once upon a time in Ghana, a British Governor, Sir Frederick Hodgson, desired to plonk his plump posterior on the Ashanti's sacred Golden Stool, on behalf of the Queen. This is how the idiotic Governor addressed the Ashanti chiefs:

'What must I do to the man, whoever he is, who has failed to give to the Queen, who is the paramount power in the country, the stool to which she is entitled? Where is the Golden Stool? Why am I not sitting on the Golden Stool at this moment? I am the representative of the paramount power in this country; why have you relegated me to this chair? Why did you not take the opportunity of my coming to Kumasi to bring the Golden Stool and give it to me to sit upon?'

The Ashanti had heard enough from this *fualán!* War broke out and lasted for six months, leaving 2,000 Ashanti stone dead and a thousand British soldiers. I jest not. The world is full of raving lunatics such as Sir Frederick Hodgson. Lunacy sees to be a qualification for the job.

The slice of life found in the headlines reproduced here, all just from a mere couple of weeks in the second half of the month of August 2023, is a reminder of the concerns and obsessions of media, particularly in the dominant Anglophone world which sees itself as the centre of the universe.

The period covered, 11th August to the 31st August, 2023, is called the slow news season in the US, and the silly season in the UK and Ireland, *the part of the year when the Parliament and Law Courts are not s(h)itting.* From the point of view of this headline watcher, all seasons are silly seasons.

It could be a totally different world to the world we have glimpsed here through the lens of NYT headlines. Naturally! There are thousands of unreported stories out there, from thousands of places around the world. Who makes the choices? How and why? What and who is newsworthy?

We know – or we should know – that language not only reflects the world; it can create worlds. If headlines around the world bombard us, day in day out, with stories of war (deliberately ignoring the words of blessed peacemakers), are they not themselves beating the drums of war? Words can create adrenalin and cortisol in the body; they can also trigger good stuff such as dopamine and serotonin. Mantras have power. Chant and prayer and poetry can be powerful.

Irish druids could rhyme rats to death. "*I will not wish unto you . . . to be rimed to death as is said to be done in Ireland,*" says Philip Sydney in his 16th century *Defence of Poesie*. He was Sir Philip, but I have stripped him of his honours.

We often see clickbait headlines that draw us in, only to find that there was very little to the story in the first place. In fact, most headlines look somewhat like clickbait headlines once the reported event is a day or a week old.

In *Mr Cogito Reads the Newspaper* by Zbigniew Herbert, the Polish poet reads about the killing of 120 soldiers and observes, correctly:

they don't speak to the imagination –
too many of them!
the numeral zero
has changed them into an abstraction

Ireland has produced its fair share of inspiring newspaper headlines, such as one from *The Skibereen Eagle*, a small newspaper in Co. Cork, which declared that it was keeping an eye on the Czar of Russia. *The Sligo Weekender* had a headline: *Hat Found Up a Tree in Carney Village*. Then there was the *Mayo Advertiser*'s shocking front-page headline:

MASSIVE BLOW JOBS FOR BELMULLET

Roberto Bolaño would have liked that one, especially if he knew that a gigantic fish might have been involved. (*Béal* is the Irish for 'mouth' and one possible meaning of the name of the town might mean 'the mouth of a mullet'). No: on second thoughts, it smacks more of Magical Realism than *Infrarrealismo*. He'd be more into

HEADLESS BODY IN TOPLESS BAR
(*The New York Post*, 1982)

I worked for an Irish-language newspaper ANOIS (*Now*), for two years; now defunct. There was a paper called *INNIU* (*Today*), today defunct; and another one, called *Amárach* (*Tomorrow*), defunct. I wrote a play, about a newspaper, the play and the newspaper both called *Amanathar* (*The Day After Tomorrow*). Never performed. It's all so . . . so . . . defunct.

The American poet Baron Wormser has a poem with one of the longest titles I've ever seen (in the March 1984 issue of *Poetry*):

I Try To Explain To My Children A Newspaper Article That Says That According To A Computer A Nuclear War Is Likely To Occur In The Next Twenty Years

Let me try to write a longer one:

Baron Wormser . . . Are You Really A Baron? In My Pre-Teen Years I Played The Baron In The Operetta *The Bells Of Bruges*. I Did Not Want My Daughter Nita To Marry Franz, The Old Bellmaker's Son. No One But The Count Was Ever Going To Be Good Enough For My Nita! Nita! Forgive Me! Franz, Forgive Me!

I have been asked, 'Are there many Irish-language Infrarealists?' Are there many Irish-speaking Barons? I don't know. I may be the only one. (That is to say, the only Irish-speaking Infra poet and ex-stage Baron). Just as Cathal Ó Searcaigh is the only speaker alive today of Mín 'a Leá Irish. When it dies with him, will AI be able to recreate his dialect? Or that of Maggie Howley of the Burren?

What does it feel like to be the sole member of a literary movement? *Infrarrealismo* started off with only one member, the Chilean painter, Roberto Matta (1911-2002), after his expulsion from the Surrealist movement. For three years, he was its only member: imagine! Some commentators believe that Matta got the idea of *Infrarrealismo* from Ortega y Gasset. Genug shoyn! This is not a savage detective game.

INNTI means 'in her' and is said to have sexual connotations, but may simply have been a random word chosen by poet Michael Davitt, on overhearing someone saying 'INNTI,' meaning, 'In you get,' referring to a *naomhóg*, a Kerry canoe, which is grammatically feminine.

When we graduated from Cork and moved to Dublin (as one does), Liam Ó Muirthile, Michael Davitt and myself shared an apartment. The landlord was an academic painter, Thomas Ryan (1929-2021), later President of the Royal Hibernian Academy. (Though a Republic, Ireland is still morbidly fond of its Royal this and Royal that). Ryan had a historical painting on the wall. It could have been *The Marriage of Strongbow* or

The Flight of the Earls, or did it depict one of those many medieval battles that we lost? Thomas was surprised by our lack of interest, but we were not interested in moaning battles lost but gazing into the black sun of the future.

Ryan died in 2021, in his 92nd year, outliving two of his tenants, Davitt and Ó Muirthile. Looking back, I know why I detested his work: the historic scenes represented a Gaelic Ireland but Ryan, a Limerick man, could not communicate in the language which his historical figures once spoke and which was the adopted language of his three tenants. I hadn't the insight then to confront him and say, 'We are the Infras: we have come to revise history and destroy karma!"

Ryan considered us to be irrelevant. Progressives in the art world considered Ryan to be irrelevant. What a situation to be in, a situation, alas, repeated over and over and over again, threatening stultification, until I decided to sell my soul and enter a competition which, thanks to a piece of doggerel, won a trip around the world for myself and my wife Eithne; in our first port of call, Kerala, in the south of India, light entered my soul and all those lost battles of Ireland turned to victories.

There were always poems lying around in Ryan's spacious apartment. I saw one by Liam. It didn't have a title. Liam was fond of a word which he pronounced 'scúite', the past participle of 'scamh', which was given as 'scafa' in the dictionary and which could mean, among other things, 'exfoliated'. He was getting on my nerves with this newly-discovered word, using it as often as he could, so that he wouldn't forget it, and adding a touch of nasalisation to the word which I thought was unbecoming.

I put a title on the poem, *An Plibín Scúite* ('The Exfoliated Penis') and sent it off to a conservative magazine, guessing correctly that the editor might not know what it meant, but would be grateful to receive a poem – any poem – from the rising generation. It was published very soon afterwards. Liam didn't talk to me for a long time after that . . . possibly a day and a half.

We were feeling our way with hits and misses and now, almost a half a century later, I'm trying to continue where we left off. Get it out of my system. Or into my system? Man alive! What system? There is no in. No out. The solar system . . . TAT TVAM ASI!

I'll never forget an Infra-like moment in the Damer Theatre in Dublin. They had come to listen to the 'new poetry' in Irish. I asked Michael Davitt what was he going to read. He showed me a few poems. I scanned them briefly. No, I said. These people need to be shocked out of their Irish-language-revival-feigned-enthusiasm. They need to be asked some serious questions. A ferocious kick in their Sir Frederick Hodgson-like rear is what they need in order to come out of their cultural coma, their complacency. Here, I said, handing him a poem I had been studying at the time. This is what you will read!

Davitt went out on the stage and, looking boldly at a sea of bewildered faces, intoned *The Akond Of Swot,* stanza by cruel stanza, to the bitter end. It wasn't the poem itself but the fact that it was in English which nearly caused a riot:

> WHO, or why, or which, or what,
> Is the Akond of Swat?
> Is he tall or short, or dark or fair?
> Does he sit on a stool or a sofa or chair,
> OR SQUAT?
> The Akond of Swat?
> Is he wise or foolish, young or old?
> Does he drink his soup or his coffee cold,
> OR HOT,
> The Akond of Swat?
> Does he sing or whistle, jabber or talk,
> And when riding abroad does he gallop or walk,
> OR TROT,
> The Akond of Swat?
> Does he wear a turban, a fez or a hat?
> Does he sleep on a matress, a bed, or a mat,
> OR A COT,
> The Akond of Swat? . . .

And so on . . . Funnily enough, he never came up in conversation after that – not once – the Akond of Swat.

Tristan Tzara was always resigning from Dada. I'm not surprised. The word 'dada' in Modern Irish means 'nothing': 'níl dada ann' = *it amounts to nothing!* Nothing! In Middle Irish it meant something – a mote in a sunbeam.

If I resign from the Irish Infrarealist movement (Infreareálachas) which I've just founded – a distinct possibility, I might add – I may well skedaddle before anyone even gets to know of its existence in the first place.

That kind of thing has happened before. A number of haiku stalwarts got together to form a society known as An Cumann Um Haiku and an American haiku master James W. Hackett presented signed copies of his books to our august society when he visited Ireland on my invitation. A couple of unspeakable things occurred that took the wind out of our sails and the society never recovered. So, you could say it was a goner before it ever got started.

Will this be the fate of *Infrarrealismo* in Ireland? Should I be worried? There are more serious things to be worried about, according to *The New York Times*. Such as? Days on Mars getting shorter.

If I do resign, will it be in high dudgeon, or despair? Or sheer perversity? *Infrarrealismo!* Jaysus! How did I get to be here? Well, in my green and salad days, I had an interest in anthropology which taught me one thing: how arrogant we are in our manners and ways; as if there's only one way of behaving, one way of living, one way of writing, one way of speaking, one way of thinking and looking at the world.

This is the root cause of my eternal blossoming, into one thing and another: today it's *Infrarrealismo/ Infrearéalachas*. Tomorrow? I don't know. I feel I am alone in an anthropological laboratory, working day and night, with no one to say if an experiment is going badly wrong, or not. If I'm arrested, and protest, saying 'I'm looking for the wrinkles on Mahākāśyapa"s face!', can I expect much sympathy? Or, 'I'm looking for the face of one of the Ancient Ones, the *Kiash Matchitiwuk!*' Or, to quote Yeats, *'I'm looking for the face I had before the world was made.'* Invalid search, that's what I'll be told.

In Part Two of Jack Foley's 83rd Birthday Show, on 16th August 2023, Jack announced that 'the aliveness that I associated with the intense experience of poetry thrust me into a larger world – a world in which the solidity of "I" disappeared and moved me in various directions.' One thinks of Whitman: "Do I contradict myself? / Very well then, I contradict myself, / (I am large, I contain multitudes.)"

Ignacio Lopez-Calvo in his book on Roberto Bolaño, *Critical Insights (Salem Press, 2016)*, describes his subject as driven to destroy the existing canon – Magical Realism and everything else that came out of South America – by sheer dint of *Infrarrealismo,* and describes Bolaño in a wonderful phrase as 'the last dodo of a way of writing literature in our language.'

There are no rules, Bolaño declared: "Tell that stupid Arnold Bennett that all his rules about plot only apply to novels that are copies of other novels."

What is all this Swiftian sæva indignatio, pray? Biddy Jenkinson says:

"The poet is by profession a troublemaker. She must be independent to the point of eccentricity and is often, though not necessarily, as curst as a crow-trodden hen and as odd as one of the triple-faced monsters with which the Celts depicted Ogma the omniscient, gazing in all directions at once." (Quoted in the Editorial of *Poetry Ireland Review*, No. 140).

José Vicente Anaya wrote an Infra manifesto in 1975, stating something which needs to be repeated today, namely:

"Sanity and common sense destroy the imagination of the human being and reduce it to an objective plane in which it remains daily reproducing a miserable life; the individual is crushed by his own impotence and conformism . . ."

Discover the Infras and you will discover the power of poetry which one of the founders, Rubén Medina, explains as follows – truths that many poets have forgotten:

'It is the way in which we decide to live, communicate, think, understand each other. Poetry is the heart of the revolt, of the revolution. It is in the centre of everything. We have a poetic vision of life, not dreamy or romantic, but authentic, complex and intense. Poetry is not just what you write on a piece of paper, poetry is this moment, and understanding life like this requires you to be more critical of poses, deceit, artificiality, it requires a certain truth, a certain authenticity'.

Is it too soon for Infrearéalachas to have some impact on Irish-language poetry? Or too late? Maybe I'll put a little announcement in *The New York Times*:

Infrearéalachas (11.8. 23 – 31.8.23)

RIP

Saludos! I salute you, Infras!

Appendix (1)

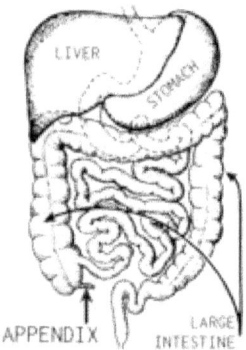

(https://commons.wikimedia.org/wiki/File:Appendix_(PSF).png)

Appendix (2)
The Bounce-Back Effect (Haibun)

When 200 Irish-language poets signed a petition and went on strike, nobody believed it. Well, nobody even got to hear about it.

Why didn't the story get out? Firstly, apart from the 200 poets in question, nobody believed that there could possibly be 200 Irish-language poets alive today. (Half of the 200 poets didn't think the other half were poets at all, and vice versa; but that's a story for another time).

Secondly, why bother to strike? How could such action have any possible effect on anyone? It would be a different story if, say, breweries and bakeries went on strike. But poets? Irish-language poets?

The truth of the matter is this: yes, there are 200 Irish-language poets, alive and well. (Let's just say 'alive' and leave it at that). I saw the list and can account for most of them. 200. Apart from the lone wolves. Lone wolves sign nothing, do nobody's bidding. Nobody gets to know them. They flee familiarity, retreating into the magnificent, indescribable matrix of their own dialect and folklore, their own obscure but chastening view of history and modernity.

> some still hear
> her terrible wail
> the last wolf in Ireland

> cloistear fós an t-olagón
> an mac tíre deireanach
> in Éirinn

Many of the 200 poets were puzzled that their action was completely ignored, apart from a few tweets among themselves that went unnoticed. (If they were on strike, they shouldn't have been tweeting). They began to regret the whole business and blamed the instigator of the strike, a maverick who was once accused in the monthly magazine *Comhar* of informing his readers what he had eaten for breakfast that morning; thereupon, the said so-called maverick brought out a slim volume of poems called *Calóga Arbhair*, meaning 'cornflakes', and got some of his cronies to write predictable blurbs, such as (I translate):'crunchy', 'nutritious' and so on. One of his cronies, who couldn't think of anything to say, sent him an emoji and that, too, was duly slapped on to the back of the book, along with all the other corny endorsements. What's the world coming to? Poems about cornflakes? Emojis? Maybe it's the readers who should go on strike.

Anyway, I wanted to know why the story couldn't find any traction in the media. I didn't expect coverage in *The New York Times*, but why is it that Irish media ignored the strike? I half-knew a sub-editor in the *Sunday Independent* and worked up the courage to ask her why the newspaper didn't think the story was newsworthy. A lot of humming and hawing and then, finally, she said, 'We had to think of the bounce-back effect.'
Bounce-back effect? She explained. 'It could have bounced back on us. 200 poets on strike. If we reported that, we'd have to report on your grievances and, as you know, the media contribute to what you see as your neglect, your isolation. An average of three books in a decade from each of these poets; that's 600 books, right? Nobody has seen any of these books – I certainly haven't – but I'm pretty sure they exist, somewhere, in some parallel universe. OK?'

'Yeah,' I said, weakly.

'We didn't want to be accused of not having reviewed any of them – not a single title – your own included, I might add. 600 unreviewed books? It wouldn't look good. And that's just the poetry! So, I'm afraid, there you have it. It's a vicious circle. We don't want to admit that we don't have sufficient proficiency in the language to read literature in Irish, or comment upon it in any way. You didn't hear this from me, but that's why the story of the strike was unceremoniously binned as non-newsworthy. There *was* a story there to be sure, but the bounce-back effect was the deciding factor.'

'The bounce-back effect . . .'

'Yup! There's constant rivalry in media circles – sure – but we know when to circle the wagons when we have to. Gottit?'

mionchrith talún
sa tSile
níor gortaíodh éinne

small earthquake
in Chile
nobody hurt

Appendix (3)

On page 1
a report of the killing of 120 soldiers . . .

    close alongside
    news of a sensational crime
    with a mugshot of the murderer, etc. etc.

    (from *Mr Cogito Reads the Newspaper* by Zbigniew Herbert)

Poetry Titles from Gabriel Rosenstock
(An updated selection)

Boatman! take these songs from me
(Tanka in response to artwork by Masood Hussain)
Manipal Universal Press, India 2023

Love Letter to Kashmir
(Tanka & Haiku in response to watercolours by Masood Hussain)
Cross-Cultural Communications, NY, 2023

Garsún: Boy (A memoir in verse)
Translated from the Irish by Paddy Bushe
Arlen House, Ireland, 2023

Stirrings of Love (Tanka)
Irish, English, Japanese, Romanian and Greek
Junpa Books, Japan, 2023

Orang-Utan (Haiku for Children 8-12 +)
FreeKidsBooks.org 2023

Conversations with Li He
Translated from the Irish by Garry Bannister
Cross-Cultural Communications, NY, 2021

Glengower (Poems for No One in Irish and English)
The Onslaught Press 2018

The Stars Are His Bones
Upanishadic Photo-Haiku with Debiprasad Mukherjee
Cross-Cultural Communications, NY, 2021

Cuach Ó Aois Eile Ag Glaoch
Coiscéim 2014

Scairt Feithide (Versions of Korean poet Ko Un)
An Sagart 2012

Rúnimirce an Anama (Versions of Macedonian poet
Nikola Madzirov)
Coiscéim 2010

Gaotha ar Fán (Versions of Pakistani poet Munir Niazi)
Coiscéim 2006

An Spealadóir Polannach (Versions of German poet
Peter Huchel)
Comhar 1994

*Cruth an Daonnaí: De vorm van een mens (*Versions of Flemish poet
Willem M. Roggeman)

Coiscéim 1990

    (More titles listed on WorldCat.org)

About the Author

(Photo: IMRAM Irish-language literature festival)

Gabriel Rosenstock is a poet, tankaist, haikuist, children's author, playwright, essayist, short story writer, novelist, translator and in the words of Hugh MacDiarmid, 'a champion of forlorn causes'.

About Revival Press

"A good poem shocks us awake, one way or another - through its beauty, its insight, its music; it shakes or seduces the reader out of the common gaze and into a genuine looking. And make no mistake I consider such a moment of transformation to be a radical event."

— *Jane Hirshfield*

Revival Press is a community publishing press and is the poetry imprint of The Limerick Writers' Centre. It was founded by managing editor Dominic Taylor in 2007. It grew out of the Revival Poetry Readings established in Limerick 2003 by Barney Sheehan and Dominic Taylor. It has published over fifty poetry titles to date.

Revival has also helped establish a number of local and national poets by publishing their first collections.

One of the aims of Revival Press is to make writing and publishing both available and accessible to all. It tries as much as possible to represent diverse voices and advocates for increased writing and publishing access to individuals and groups that have not typically had this access.

It continues to represent local authors and to offer advice and encouragement to aspiring writers.

Revival Press supports Fair Trade Publishing.

www.ingramcontent.com/pod-product-compliance
Lightning Source LLC
Chambersburg PA
CBHW072214070526
44585CB00015B/1337